HA SC VEN ES

D1605206

INTERWEAVE PRESS

Project editor, Judith Durant
Selection editors, Jean Scorgie, Marilyn Murphy, Linda Ligon,
    Dawn Hamilton, Judith Durant, Ann Budd
Technical editor, Jane Fournier
Photography, Joe Coca
Photo styling, Judith Durant
Cover design, Bren Frisch
Page design, Dean Howes, Andy Webber

Interweave Press
201 East Fourth Street
Loveland, Colorado 80537 USA
www.interweave.com

Printed in Singapore by Tien Wah Press

Library of Congress Cataloging-in-Publication Data

Handwoven scarves/from the editors of Handwoven.
        p. cm.
    ISBN 1-883010-65-9
        1. Hand weaving—Patterns. 2. Scarves—United States.

    TT848 .H3577 1999
    746.1'40432—dc21   99-046597

10 9 8 7 6 5 4 3

Preface

This scarf. This long narrow tidy rectangle, cut just now from the loom: stiff, geometric, proper. Warps, longitudinal. Wefts, lateral. Just so. But finish the fringes, trim the loose ends, give it a gentle wash and press, and watch it take on a life of its own.

Watch it ripple, undulate, shimmer, insinuate itself into an intimate wearable sculpture. Watch it catch the light; watch its subtle pattern emerge, fade. Watch the magic.

What's simpler to weave than a scarf? So few warp ends, so straightforward in the weaving and finishing. Yet what's more versatile? You can weave a soft, wooly, nappy scarf to warm against the vulpine winds of winter. You can weave a diaphanous, silky, seductive scarf to conceal or reveal, as you choose. You can make a fashion statement, or you can create a comfy old friend.

You can consider each new scarf a sampler, a testing ground for color, texture, weave structure. After all, you will have invested so relatively little in time and materials. You can put on a long, long warp and weave every scarf to a different tune. You can learn. From your scarves.

You can gift your friends, endlessly. Who ever has too many scarves, after all? Who doesn't need a scarf of fourteen blues for those blue, blue eyes, or a scarf of gypsy fringe and hue to make each day a little, just a little, crazy? And if you weave this scarf with tidy, mitered hems, what if you weave it again with cascades of sparkling beads? How can you stop? Weaving? These scarves?

You have the tools. You have the wit, the taste, the patience, you even have the time. Really you do. And heaven knows, you have the yarn. And with this book, you have the inspiration, too, if that has somehow been lacking. So weave a scarf. Join the weavers whose wonders are shown in this book. Give yourself the joy.

Linda

Linda Ligon, Founder and President, Interweave Press
August, 1999

Contents

Scarf on previous page by Laura Fry.
See pages 36–37 for details.

Introduction

Faced with the task of collecting fifty of the greatest scarves ever woven, the craft editors at Interweave Press got together as a group to figure out how to proceed. It quickly became apparent that we could only come up with fifty of the greatest scarves ever woven *by weavers known to us.* Well, that's how it had to be, and we scoured our rolodexes for a list of weavers whose work we know and like. It then became apparent that we would end up with some of the greatest scarves ever woven *by weavers known to us* and *in their opinion.* So we thought, at the very least, we'd ask our weaver friends for one to four samples of their work. We composed a solicitation letter, merged it with our list of weavers, and were on our way. As fortune would have it, one weaver spoke with another, and we heard from artisans not in our rolodexes. We welcomed their submissions along with the others.

Soon enough, in a way that still seems magical even to this group of veteran editors, packages began arriving. And these packages were filled with wonderful surprises. We had piles of scarves in many shapes and sizes, imaginative color schemes, unusual fiber combinations, and striking weave structures. The scarves were small and lightweight, fashioned to wear as indoor accessories. The scarves were huge and heavy, made to fend off harsh winter weather. The scarves were subtly shaded with fine lines of pattern, inviting closer inspection. The scarves were bright and bold, not to be missed from half a mile away. The scarves were angora, with a soft and fuzzy aura. The scarves were tightly woven silk, with smooth, slick surfaces. The scarves were doublewoven with shifting layers of pattern and color. The scarves were structured in novel ways, producing interesting texture when washed. Most of all, the scarves were unique, each and every one the product of a talented designer who is also an accomplished artisan.

Then came the hard part. Choosing fifty. We tried not to be too intellectual, not worrying too much about selecting a balanced number of large and small, bright and demure, wool and silk, 4-shaft and multi-shaft. Rather, we selected scarves that made us say "Wow!" The Wow! may have been prompted by a high number of ends per inch, an unlikely but successful color combination, or simply a certain *je ne sais quoi.* We selected scarves that we'd like to own—and scarves we'd like to weave. And because we couldn't narrow it down to exactly fifty, you'll actually find fifty-two scarves by twenty-eight weavers.

We asked the participants to include as much information about their scarves as they felt comfortable sharing. In most cases, you'll find finished size, fabric description, warp and weft materials, project notes, and a draft. In some cases you'll find more, in others, less. We hope that in every case you'll find a scarf that inspires you weave your own version of the world's greatest scarf.

Northern Lights Silk Scarf

SHARON ALDERMAN

Finished size: 10" × 80" including fringe.

Fabric description: Block twill.

Warp: Plied silk in navy; handspun silk in variegated turquoise, purple, and pink.

Weft: Plied silk in navy.

Project notes: This classic block twill shows a little of a special yarn to good advantage. The variegated handspun yarn is randomly distributed in the warp and makes up only ¼ of the number of warp ends. The single navy weft shuttle makes weaving fast and easy.

There are eight wide and seven narrow blocks across the warp. The fringe is enhanced with iridescent beads slipped onto the warp ends before they were twisted into fringe.

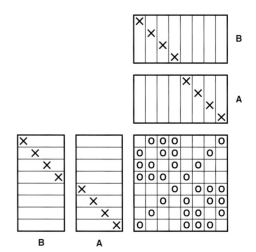

Sharon Alderman has been weaving nearly every day since 1970. She teaches and lectures throughout the United States, Canada, and the United Kingdom. Her writing and work have appeared in Shuttle, Spindle, & Dyepot; Interweave; Textile Artist's Newsletter; Weaver's; *and* Handwoven—*where she is a Contributing Editor. Her books include* Handwoven, Tailormade, *and* A Handweaver's Notebook *both published by Interweave Press, Inc.*

Dyed Block Twill Scarf

KATHY BRIGHT

Finished size: 8½" × 66" plus fringe.

Fabric description: Block twill.

Warp: 20/2 silk, silk/rayon, and rayon/silk noil painted in purple, pink, and yellow.

Weft: 20/2 silk in gray.

E.P.I.: 24.

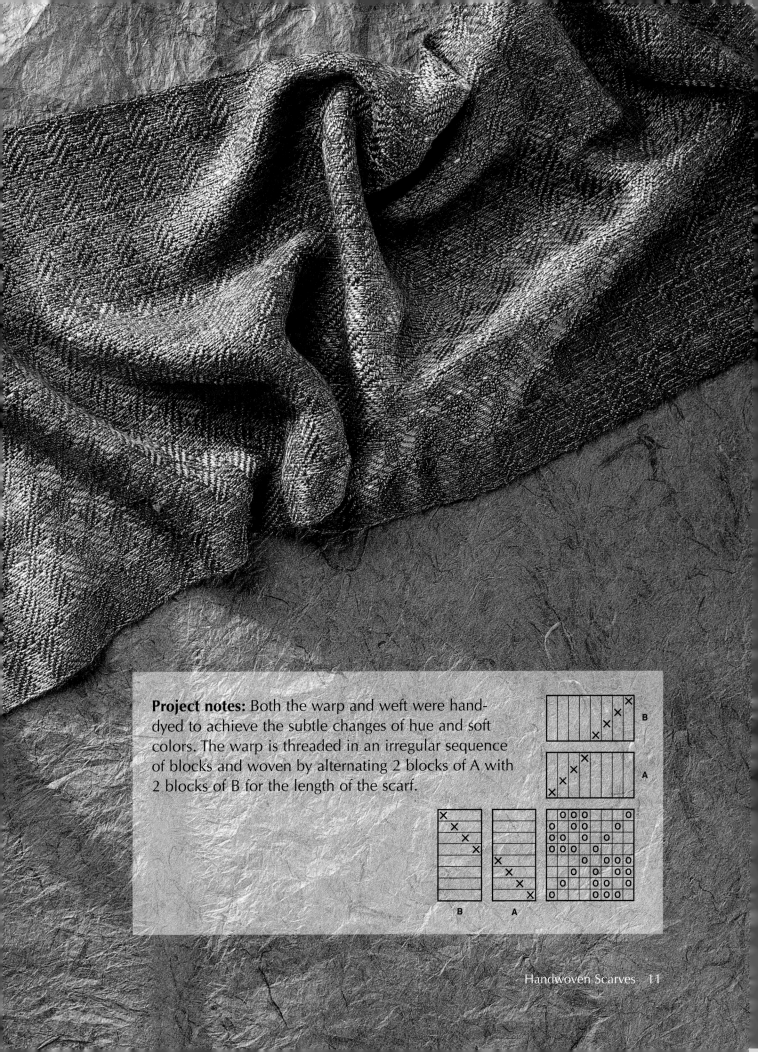

Project notes: Both the warp and weft were hand-dyed to achieve the subtle changes of hue and soft colors. The warp is threaded in an irregular sequence of blocks and woven by alternating 2 blocks of A with 2 blocks of B for the length of the scarf.

Black Supplementary Warp Scarf

Kathy Bright

Finished size: 9¼" × 69" plus fringe.

Fabric description: Plain weave with supplementary warp bands.

Warp and weft: 18/2 wool/silk blend in black; fine metallic thread.

plain weave incorporates supplementary warp

supplementary warp floats above plain weave

supplementary warp floats below plain weave

● = supplementary warp

supplementary warp band

plain weave

Supplementary warp: 18/2 wool/silk blend in purple, turquoise, and royal blue.

E.P.I.: 20 for the plain weave, 40 (20 background and 20 supplementary) for the supplementary warp bands.

Project notes: The plain weave background of this fabric is threaded on shafts 1 and 2, and the supplementary warp bands on harness 3. When weaving this type of fabric it's important to begin and end the scarf with plain weave incorporating the supplementary warp and to keep the warp floats short so that they're not vulnerable to snagging.

Navy Supplementary Warp Scarf

Kathy Bright

Finished size: 8½" × 68" plus fringe.

Fabric description: Plain weave with supplementary warp bands.

Warp and weft: 18/2 silk/wool blend in navy.

Supplementary warp: 18/2 silk/wool blend in medium blue and light blue.

E.P.I.: 20 for the plain weave, 40 (20 background and 20 supplementary warp) for the supplementary warp bands.

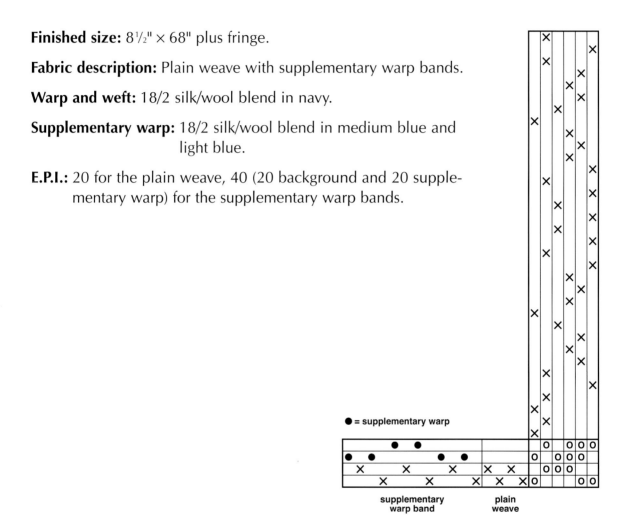

● = supplementary warp

supplementary warp band

plain weave

Kathy Bright *and her family share their Pennsylvania farm with sixty llamas. She has been an active weaver and spinner for twenty-five years and is currently owner of a weaving and spinning shop called Indian Hills Handwovens.*

Thick, Thinner, Thinnest or Thin, Thicker, Thickest

Erica de Ruiter

Finished size: 7" × 70" including fringe.

Fabric description: Log cabin plain weave.

Warp and weft: 20/2 cotton in blue and orange.

E.P.I.: 16 working ends.

P.P.I.: 16.

Project notes: Using only 2 shafts, the subtle color shadings in this scarf are the result of gradually changing the relative thickness of warp and weft colors. The changing thickness is achieved by bundling more than one thread as a working end. The weave and fabric is balanced overall because the total number of threads in any adjacent pair of working ends or picks is always 6. The numbers next to the color in the draft indicate how many strands make up the working end or pick. Weaving requires ten shuttles, five for each color with a different number of strands wound together on each shuttle.

Two-Layered Scarf with Shifted Layers

ERICA DE RUITER

Finished size: 6¼" × 54½" including fringe.

Fabric description: Doubleweave with lengthwise plain weave borders.

Warp and weft: 36/2 merino wool; layer A in purples, blue, and green; layer B in yellows, oranges, blue, and green.

E.P.I.: 30 for plain weave borders, 60 (30 per layer) for doubleweave.

P.P.I.: 30.

Project notes: There are two wefts for this fabric. They weave from opposite sides part way across the warp, weaving doubleweave where they overlap. A purple weft weaves layer A and a yellow weft weaves layer B. The borders at each end of the scarf are made up of treadling blocks A, B, and C. The body of the scarf uses treadling blocks D, C, and A.

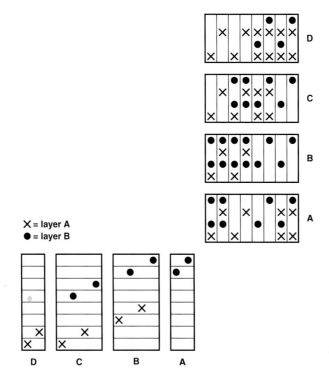

X = layer A
● = layer B

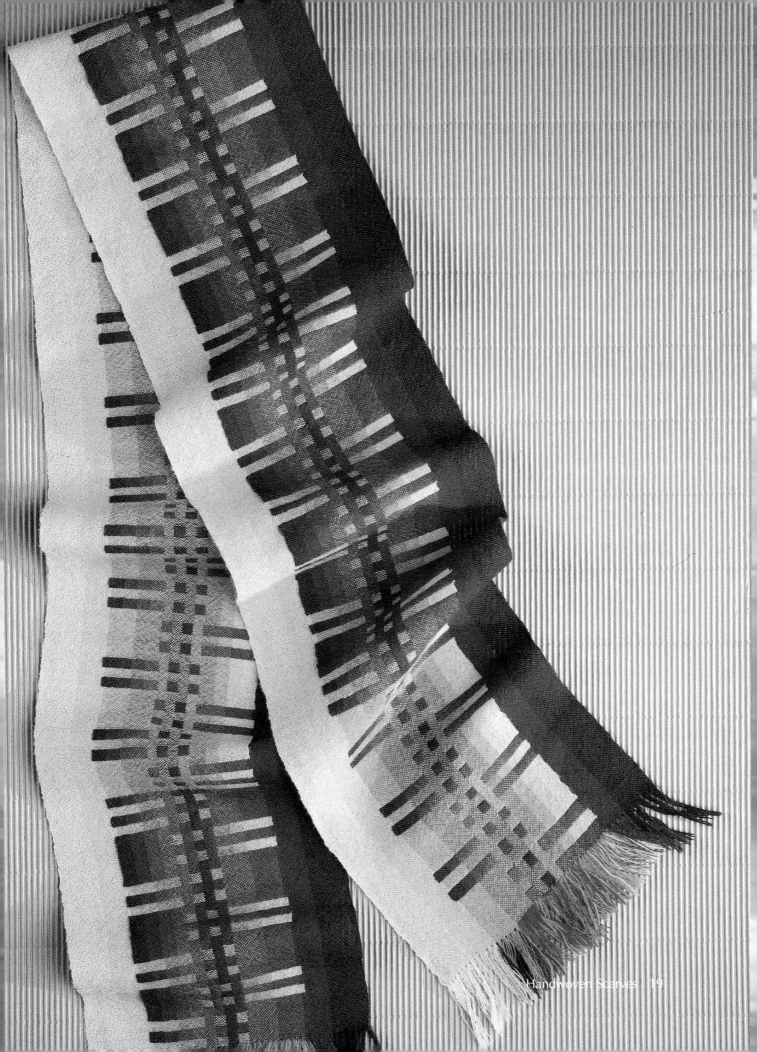

Natural and Terra Cotta

Erica de Ruiter

Finished size: 6½" × 75½" including fringe.

Fabric description: Log cabin plain weave.

Warp and weft: 2-ply silk in terra-cotta and ecru.

E.P.I.: 16 working ends.

P.P.I.: 16.

Project notes: This scarf is woven using the same draft as the scarf on pages 16–17. The technique is most effective when the colors contrast strongly.

Erica de Ruiter lives in Amsterdam and has worked for many years as a designer for the textile industry. She has been teaching handweaving for the last twenty years. Erica specializes in two- and three-shaft weaving structures and has published several books on handweaving in Dutch.

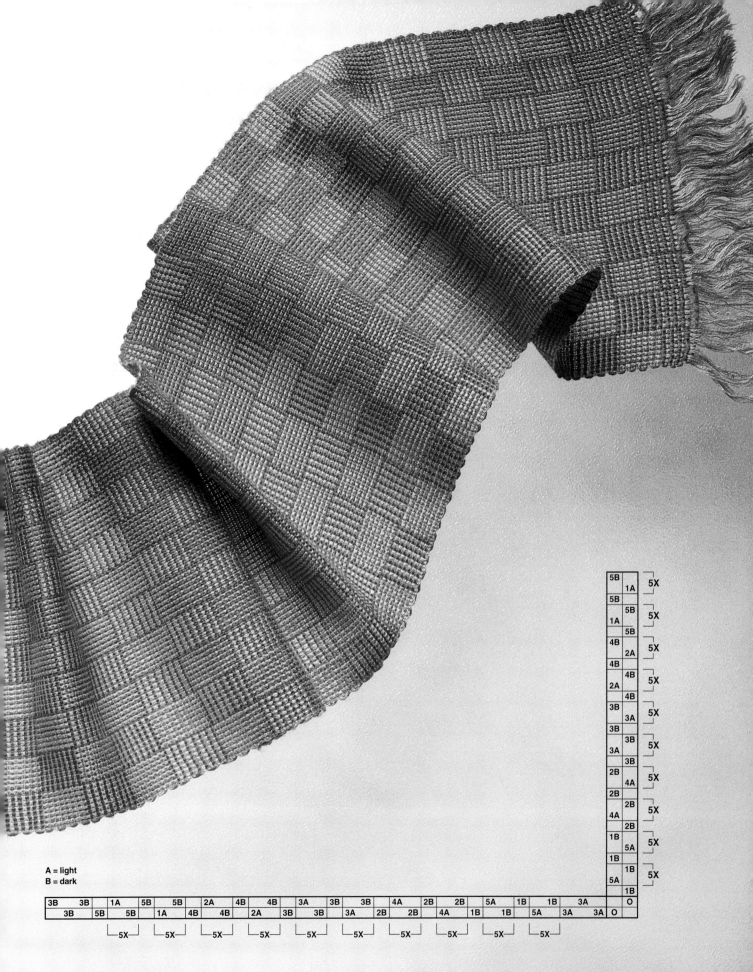

A = light
B = dark

Drawloom Damask Scarf

E. Del Zoppo

Finished size: 7" × 57½" including fringe.

Fabric description: Broken twill damask.

Warp and weft: 30/2 silk.

E.P.I.: 37½.

Project notes: This is a scarf from my standard repertoire—my bread and butter line of scarves. It's drawloom damask on a shaft draw system. The pattern threading is straight draw on 10 shafts with 4-end units and 6 repeats. The border threading is straight draw on 4 shafts with 4-end units. The ground threading is straight draw on 4 shafts. The treadling is broken twill.

Damask Ribbons

E. Del Zoppo

Finished size: 7" × 56" including fringe.

Fabric description: Broken twill damask.

Warp: 60/2 silk.

Weft: Singles douppioni silk.

E.P.I.: 80.

Project notes: This scarf is a prototype for a planned run of special scarves I was going to produce with finer thread and more complex patterning. That fine thread really let me play with the damask and the idea of a length of ribbons bound together by pattern and weft. It is drawloom damask on a shaft draw system. The pattern threading is on 67 shafts with 4-end units. The border threading is on 3 shafts with 4-end units. The ground threading is straight draw on 4 shafts. The treadling is broken twill.

Big Scarf

E. Del Zoppo

Finished size: 19½" × 79" including fringe.

Fabric description: Satin damask.

Warp: 30/2 silk.

Weft: Tram silk used 6 strands together.

E.P.I.: 37½.

Project notes: This is my scarf of choice when I want a lot of fabric for warmth or just a bit of quiet drama. I love the effect of navy blue on black; the ribboned areas are broken by the pattern and seem to dive in and out of the darkness on one side, while the pattern floats over them on the other. I want my scarves to be as interesting while they are being worn as when they are hanging for display. And I want them to merit closer examination by the wearer as well as by others. This is draw-loom damask on a shaft draw system. The pattern threading is straight draw on 66 shafts with 5-end units and 2 repeats. The border threading is straight draw on 4 shafts with 5-end units. The ground threading is straight draw on 5 shafts. The treadling is 5-shaft satin.

E. Del Zoppo lives on Cape Breton Island, Nova Scotia. She works in a seaside studio on the Atlantic and spends part of each winter in Jamaica.

Pleated Scarf

GISELA EVITT

Finished size: *7" × 75"* including fringe.

Fabric description: Block twill.

Warp: Plied silk in purple, red, gold, and pink.

Weft: High twist, singles wool in natural black.

E.P.I.: 20.

Project notes: Both this Scarf and the Smooth Scarf on page 31 were woven on the same warp but at different setts. The warp is alternating stripes with one color group threaded in block A and the other in block B. The high twist of the handspun wool weft pulls the alternating warp- and weft-dominant stripes into rounded pleats. The body of the scarf is woven in long continuous stripes of treadling block A with two small bands of block B for contrast.

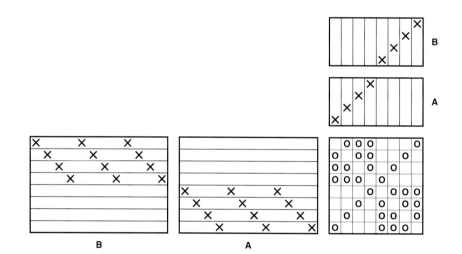

Smooth Scarf

GISELA EVITT

Finished size: 12" × 74" including fringe.

Fabric description: Block twill.

Warp: Plied silk in purple, red, gold, and pink.

Weft: Singles silk in variegated colors.

E.P.I.: 30.

Project notes: This scarf was woven on the same warp, but at a closer sett, as the Pleated Scarf on page 29. The weft was handspun from painted silk top. The treadling produces alternating blocks of weft- and warp-dominant twill.

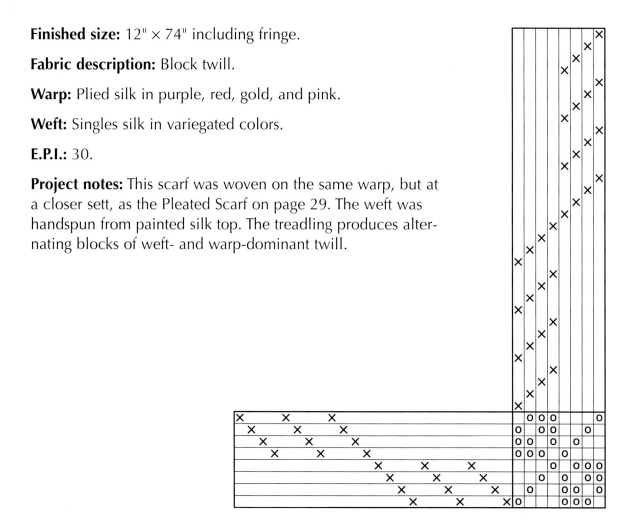

Rippling Water

GISELA EVITT

Finished size: 11" × 87½" including fringe.

Fabric description: Plain weave.

Warp: 20/2 mercerized cotton in medium blue.

Weft: 20/2 mercerized cotton, one strand each white, medium blue, and dark blue twisted together.

E.P.I.: 20.

Project notes: A fragment of old Chinese plain-weave fabric with a subtle pattern like rippling water challenged me to produce the same effect. I discovered that the pattern was the result of the interaction of multicolored twisted weft yarns. For this scarf, I twisted white, medium blue, and dark blue yarns together on my spinning wheel to make the weft. When woven, the colors in adjacent weft picks work together to create the watery pattern.

Gisela Evitt's early training as a scientist determined her "what if . . . then what?" experimental approach to spinning and weaving, which she came on accidentally while raising three sons. Exposure to nature's myriad colors honed her color sense.

Silk Cashmere Scarf

LAURA FRY

Finished size: 11½" × 54" plus fringe.

Fabric description: Block twill.

Warp: 30/2 silk in off-white; gold Mylar filament.

Weft: 2-ply cashmere in off-white.

E.P.I.: 36.

P.P.I.: 36.

Project notes: The gold Mylar is threaded along with every silk warp end on shaft 16. After a washing and a hard steam press, this scarf was very stiff. I tumbled it in the clothes dryer, without heat, for several minutes until it emerged with the softness and drape you'd expect from silk and cashmere.

Wool Gauze Scarf/Shawl

Laura Fry

Finished size: 16½" × 78" plus fringe.

Fabric description: Plain weave with warp-wise twill stripes.

Warp and weft: 40/2 worsted wool in off-white; Mylar bouclé in opalescent.

E.P.I.: 24 for threadings A and C, 32 for threading B, and 16 for threading D.

P.P.I.: 24.

Project notes: The warp for this scarf is threaded in repeats of the sequence B, C, and D, with the A threading forming each selvedge. With an 8-dent reed, I was easily able to sley each threading at a different sett, giving them each a different degree of transparency.

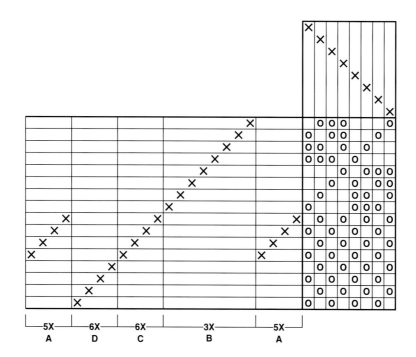

Laura Fry has been a professional/production weaver since the 1970s. She recently achieved the Master Weaver certificate as granted by the Guild of Canadian Weavers. Her monograph was on wet finishing and fulling.

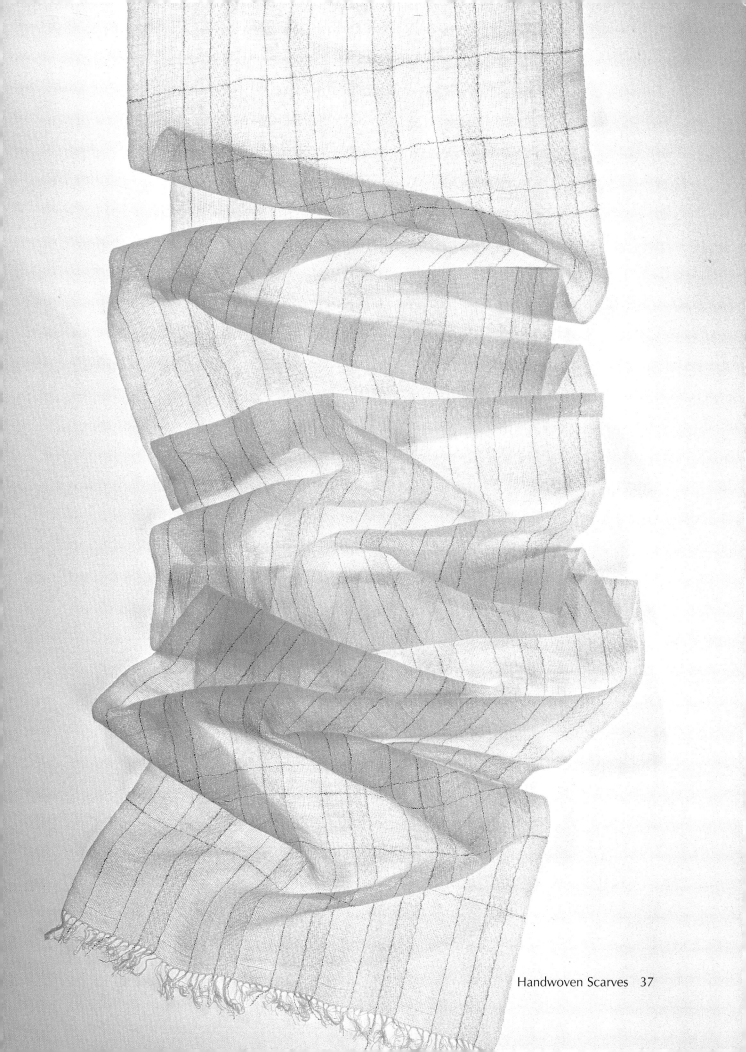

Overshot Scarf

MARGUERITE GINGRAS

Finished size: 7 ½" × 64" including fringe.

Fabric description: Overshot.

Warp and tabby weft: 20/2 mercerized cotton in black.

Pattern weft: 20/2 silk in yellow.

E.P.I.: 30.

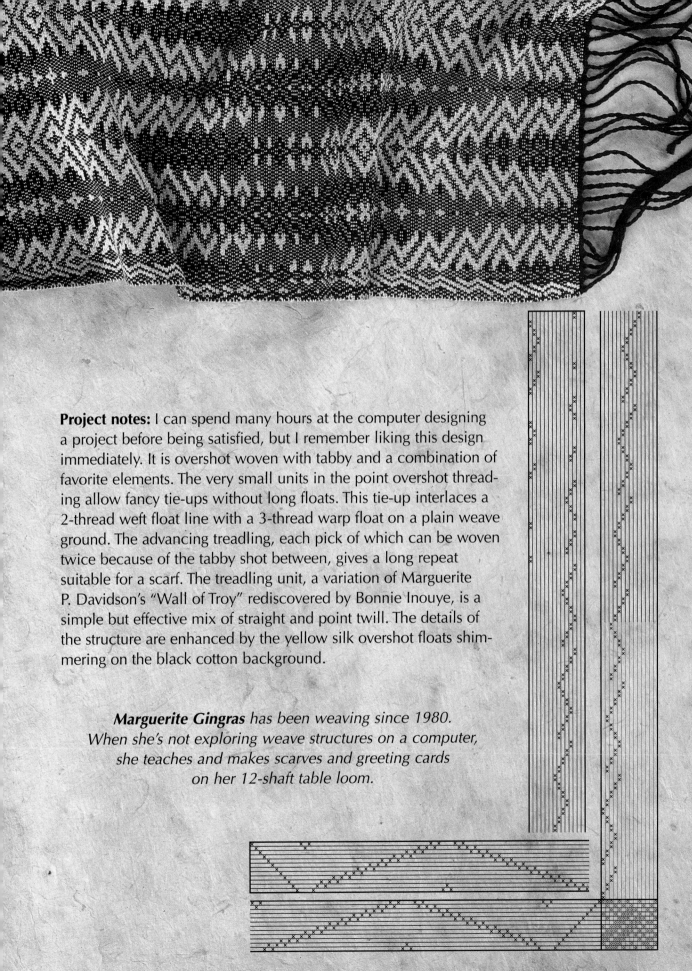

Project notes: I can spend many hours at the computer designing a project before being satisfied, but I remember liking this design immediately. It is overshot woven with tabby and a combination of favorite elements. The very small units in the point overshot threading allow fancy tie-ups without long floats. This tie-up interlaces a 2-thread weft float line with a 3-thread warp float on a plain weave ground. The advancing treadling, each pick of which can be woven twice because of the tabby shot between, gives a long repeat suitable for a scarf. The treadling unit, a variation of Marguerite P. Davidson's "Wall of Troy" rediscovered by Bonnie Inouye, is a simple but effective mix of straight and point twill. The details of the structure are enhanced by the yellow silk overshot floats shimmering on the black cotton background.

Marguerite Gingras has been weaving since 1980. When she's not exploring weave structures on a computer, she teaches and makes scarves and greeting cards on her 12-shaft table loom.

Hummingbird Scarf

BONNIE INOUYE

Finished size: 7" × 71" including fringe.

Fabric description: Twill variation.

Warp: 20/2 silk in variegated blue, purple, teal, and green.

Weft: 30/2 silk in red.

E.P.I.: 32.

Project notes: For many years I have spent the summer months in a cabin in the mountains of southwestern Colorado, an area famous for an abundance of wildflowers. My husband studies and bands hummingbirds, so I have held these iridescent marvels in my hand. I am enchanted by the way the colors dance on their tiny feathers, and have woven a series of scarves and shawls that use silk in woven iridescence.

This scarf uses yarns that I hand dyed. It has a threading that comes from the mountains outside my cabin windows and a treadling that was inspired by the spruce trees where I hunt for wild mushrooms in August.

Bonnie Inouye has been weaving since 1967. She designs on a computer, teaches workshops, writes about weaving, and sells her work in galleries.

Blue and Yellow Stripes with Beads

SONYA HASSELBERG-JOHNSON

Finished size: 7 ½" × 64" including fringe.

Fabric description: Satin.

Warp: 60/2 silk in blue and yellow.

Weft: 60/2 silk in yellow.

E.P.I.: 60.

Project notes: This scarf started as warp- and weft-dominant satin blocks pattern designed to use up an overabundance of blue and gold yarns. After a foot or so it proved extremely boring. I added random warp stripes and weft inlays and beads— I would never have designed this from scratch. It is truly a "silk purse from a sow's ear" and I love it.

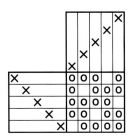

See-Through Blue

Finished size: 11" × 85".

Fabric description: Plain weave.

Warp: 30/1 S-twist and 30/1 Z-twist high-twist wool in blue.

Weft: 30/1 S-twist high-twist wool; 56/2 Z-twist high-twist wool.

E.P.I.: 30.

Project notes: I had already been working with collapse fabrics and pleating when I attended a workshop with Ann Richards. The workshop stimulated me to explore these textures further.

Sonya Hasselberg-Johnson was born and raised in Seattle and now has a professional studio near Kangarilla, South Australia. Her passion is designing, weaving, and dyeing yarns to expand the boundaries of cloth.

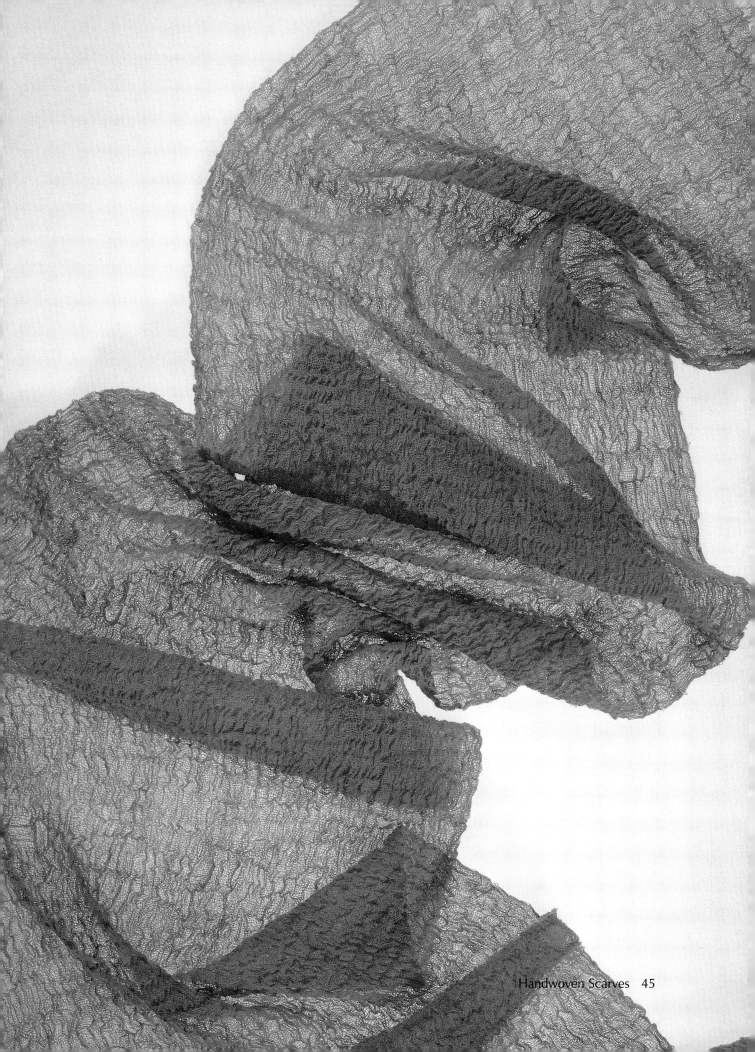

Red Pleats

TERESA KENNARD

Finished size: 36" × 103" including fringe.

Fabric description: Block twill.

Warp: 60/2 silk in red.

Weft: 120/2 silk in red.

E.P.I.: 54.

P.P.I.: 58.

Squares

TERESA KENNARD

Finished size: 8" × 83½" including fringe.

Fabric description: Block twill.

Warp: 60/2 silk in black.

Weft and weft inlay: 60/2 silk in purple, red, lavender, and white.

E.P.I.: 54.

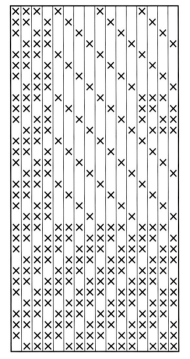

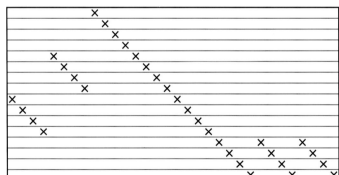

Teresa Kennard *has been weaving for the past thirteen years. Her original clothing emphasizes classic design and fine function. Teresa's garments have appeared in fashion shows and major fiber publications since 1992.*

Indigo Ikat Scarf

DAGMAR KLOS

Finished size: 7½" × 61" including fringe.

Fabric description: Point twill.

Warp: 30/2 silk in indigo with warp stripes of white-and-indigo ikat.

Weft: 30/2 silk in indigo.

E.P.I.: 36.

P.P.I.: 34.

Project notes: After winding the warp for this scarf, I selected several groups of warp threads and wrapped them at random intervals with ikat tape to create the white areas in the warp. I dyed the warp and weft to a medium shade of blue in an indigo vat. The interlocking diamonds of the point twill fabric are highlighted where the blue weft crosses the occasional bands of white warp.

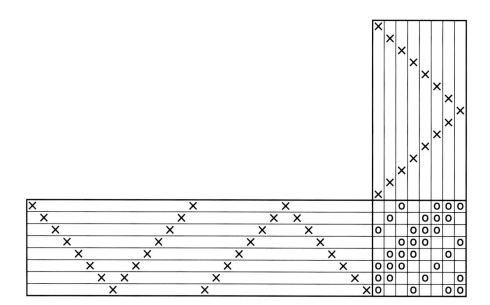

White Huck Lace Scarf

DAGMAR KLOS

Finished size: 7¾" × 67" including fringe.

Fabric description: Huck lace.

Warp and Weft: 30/2 silk in white.

E.P.I.: 33.

P.P.I.: 33.

Project notes: The sheen of silk yarn creates a play of light and shadow on the warp and weft floats of this huck lace scarf.

Since **Dagmar Klos** was a little girl, handwork has been a part of her life. Inspired by the beauty and craftsmanship of her grandmother's needlework, she has embodied that same pursuit of perfection in her handwork, especially her fine handwovens—functional pieces of art intended for everyday use.

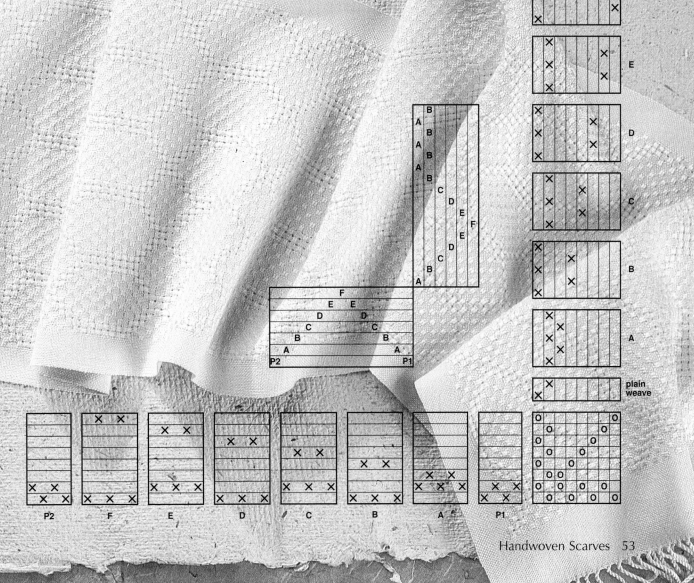

Painted Warp Scarf 1

SARA LAMB

Finished size: 8 ½" × 81" including fringe.

Fabric description: Plain weave.

Warp: 20/2 silk in red with variegated white and black warp stripes.

Weft: Fine 2-ply silk.

E.P.I.: 40.

Project notes: The visual impact for this and the following two scarves comes from the hand-dyed warps. The dyes are applied directly onto the yarns with a paintbrush and the yarns are then steamed to set the color. In assembling the warps, I use stripes of yarns that have been wound into warp then dyed, along with stripes of yarns that have been dyed before being wound into warp. Each of the scarves is woven in warp-dominant plain weave with a fine weft of one color.

Painted Warp Scarf 2

SARAH LAMB

Finished size: 9" × 78" including fringe.

Fabric description: Plain weave.

Warp: 20/2 silk in variegated orange, red, purple, and blue.

Weft: Fine 2-ply silk.

E.P.I.: 40.

Painted Warp Scarf 3

SARA LAMB

Finished size: 7" × 77½" including fringe.

Fabric description: Plain weave.

Warp: 20/2 silk in variegated yellow, orange, red, and purple.

Weft: Fine 2-ply silk.

E.P.I.: 40.

Sara Lamb has been a weaver for more than twenty years, and still tends to stick to the basics—plain weave, simple dyeing techniques, and good, sturdy, well-made cloth. She teaches weaving, dyeing, and beadwork classes, and works in her studio in Northern California.

Painted Cotton Warp Scarf

BONNIE LUCKEY

Finished size: 9¾" × 94" including fringe.

Fabric description: Twill variation.

Warp: 12/2 mercerized cotton hand-painted in blue, pink, and gold.

Weft: 20/2 silk in black.

E.P.I.: 30.

P.P.I.: 30.

Project notes: As a consequence of living through many cold Midwestern winters, I always weave my scarves very long. This allows plenty of fabric to wrap over my head or around my neck when the weather demands it.

Bonnie Luckey dyes and weaves in the basement studio of her home in rural Nebraska. Her work ranges from complex 16-harness original designs to 2-harness tapestries.

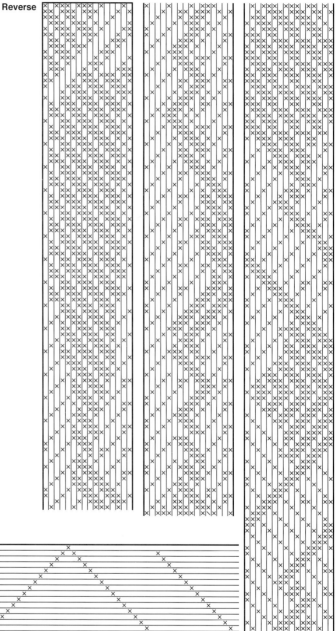

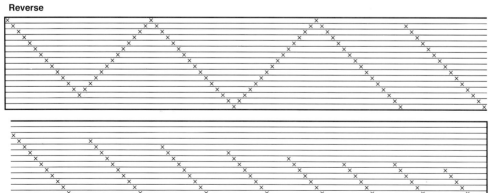

Gray Chenille

Robin Lynde

Finished size: 11" × 87" including fringe.

Fabric description: Plain weave.

Warp: Chenille in variegated khaki, olive, gray, and brown.

Weft: Rayon chenille.

Blue Chenille

ROBIN LYNDE

Finished size: 11" × 68" including fringe.

Fabric description: Plain weave.

Warp: Chenille in blue, turquoise, jade, and gray.

Weft: Chenille in royal blue.

Hot Pink Chenille

ROBIN LYNDE

Finished size: 8" × 78" including fringe.

Fabric description: Twill.

Warp: Chenille in fuchsia, black, and variegated black, fuchsia, turquoise, and purple.

Weft: Chenille in black.

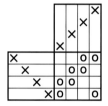

Robin Lynde lives with her three children and husband in northern California where she teaches weaving and spinning, substitute teaches, and is handy at raising sheep and dairy cows.

Golden Damask Scarves

Juul Matthijis

Finished size: *left 7" × 44", right 7" × 75"* including fringe.

Fabric description: Twill damask.

Warp: 40/2 silk used doubled.

Weft: 40/2 silk.

E.P.I.: 30.

Project notes: I wove these scarves on a 3-shaft twill threading using a damask pick-up technique developed by Erica de Ruiter of the Netherlands. It works best for designs of simple forms with bold outlines.

The background is 1/2 twill. The motifs in the left-hand scarf weave in 2/1 twill with the direction of the background and pattern twills the same. The motifs of the right-hand scarf show several different textures, each produced by altering the pick-up sequence slightly.

Juul Matthijis *was born in Rotterdam and has been weaving for twenty-five years. She now lives in the southern part of the Netherlands where she likes to weave scarves, clothing, place mats, and towels. She is also a tablet weaver and member of the weaver's guild and the tablet weaver's guild.*

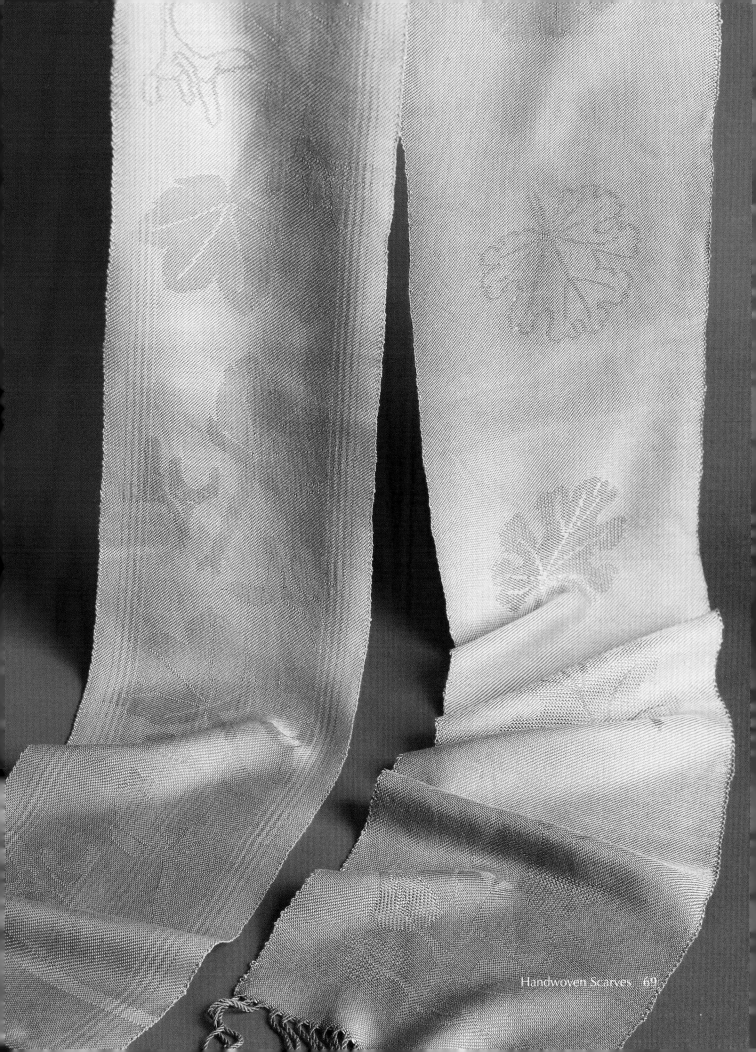

Block Twill Scarf

SELMA MIRIAM

Finished size: 10½" × 70".

Fabric description: Block twill.

Warp: Cashmere and silk cord.

Weft: Cashmere and silk ribbon.

E.P.I.: 24.

Project notes: I hand-dyed all three yarns for the scarf. The cashmere was space-dyed with logwood purple, fustic, logwood gray, and chlorophyll concentrates. Both silks were dyed logwood purple. The threading is simply alternating blocks of A and B. The treadling interposes treadling blocks A and B with occasional blocks of C and plain weave.

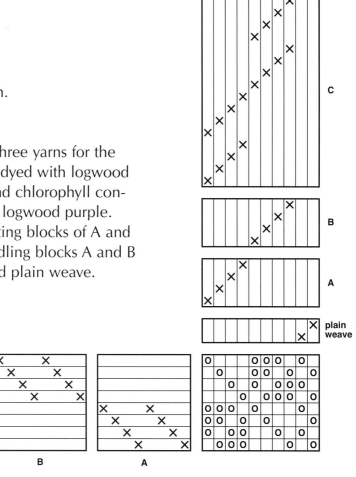

Selma Miriam owns a vegetarian restaurant and feminist bookstore called Bloodroot in Bridgeport, Connecticut, and enjoys spinning, knitting, weaving, and natural dyeing. Developing new vegetarian recipes and designing with fiber please her equally.

Cram and Space Scarf

Ann Richards

Finished size: 11" × 62" including fringe.

Fabric description: Plain weave.

Warp: Linen.

Weft: Spun silk and crepe silk.

Project notes: Narrow stripes of high-twist crepe silk and wider bands of normal-twist spun silk are used as weft across a crammed and spaced linen warp. The spacing allows the crepe yarn to collapse when washed, creating a textured stripe. There's one aspect of this type of design that I stress; only a small amount of crepe yarn is necessary to create the effect—the normal twist yarn is pushed by the crepe to give the texture.

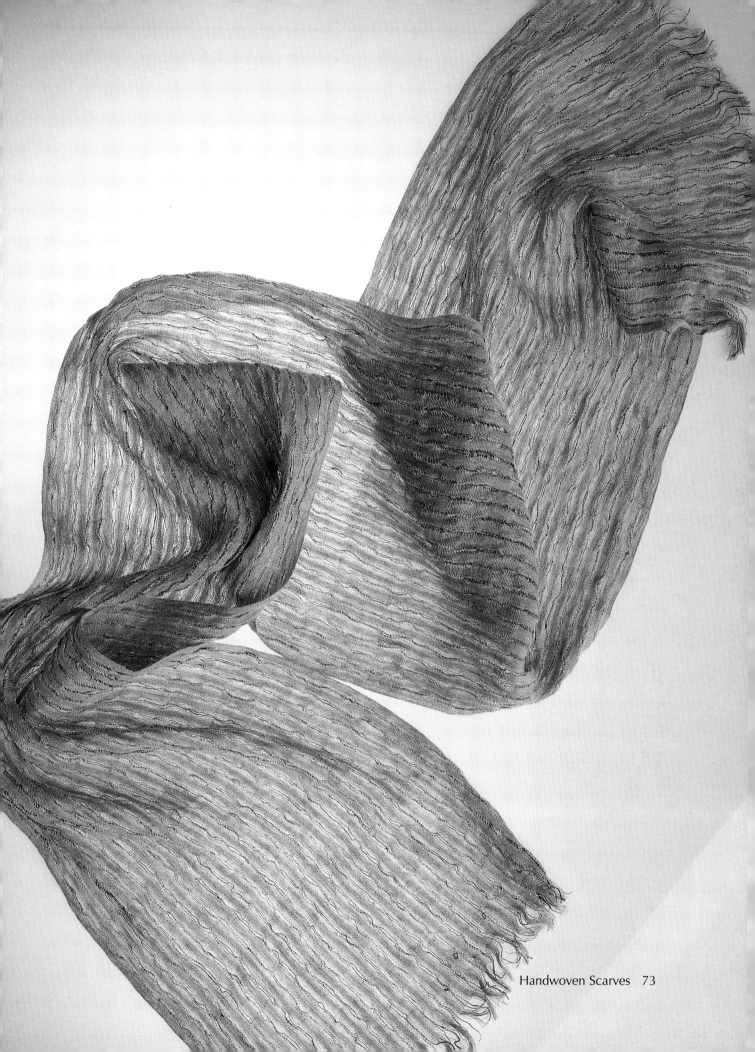

Ripplemarks

Ann Richards

Finished size: 11½" × 61" including fringe.

Fabric description: Doubleweave.

Warp: Linen.

Weft: Linen and wool crepe.

Project notes: The top layer of cloth is linen in both warp and weft, while the bottom layer has a high-twist wool crepe weft which shrinks during wet finishing. The two cloths weave together at intervals and so are braced against one another. When the bottom cloth shrinks the top cloth is thrown into relief.

*A former biologist, **Ann Richards** takes an experimental approach to weave design, using contrasts of fiber and yarn twist to create highly textured fabrics.*

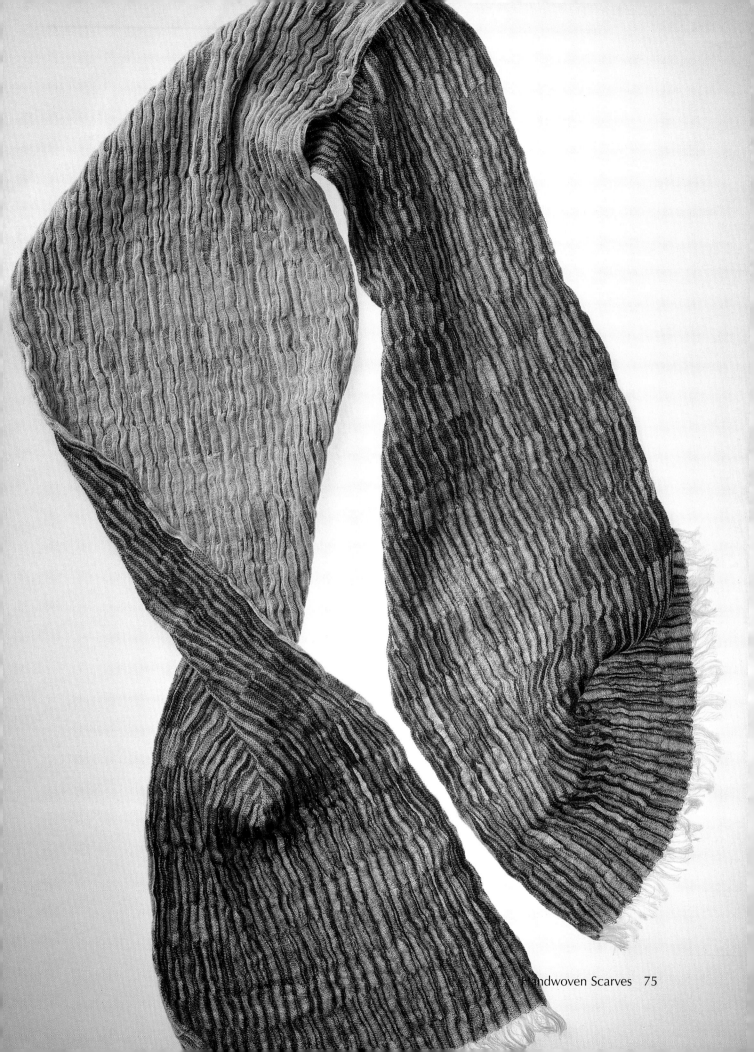

Twill Scarf

DIANA SANDERSON

Finished size: 9" × 60" including fringe.

Fabric description: Twill.

Warp: 20/2 silk cord and 15/2 tussah silk in many colors.

Weft: Fine silk bouclé in 12 colors.

E.P.I.: 30.

Project notes: The warp for the scarf is wound from yarn dyed in about 50 different graduated colors. Some groups of warp ends I selectively wrapped with ikat tape and overdyed. The treadling block sequence produces alternating 3/1 and 1/3 twill blocks and includes an occasional band of 2/2 twill.

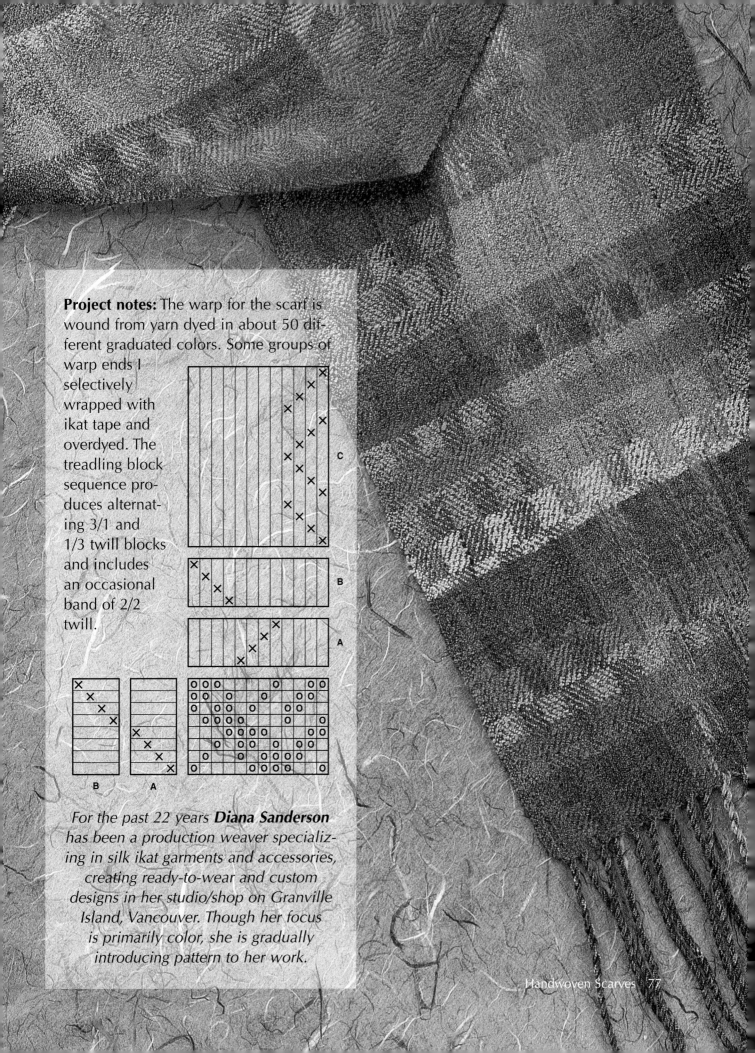

*For the past 22 years **Diana Sanderson** has been a production weaver specializing in silk ikat garments and accessories, creating ready-to-wear and custom designs in her studio/shop on Granville Island, Vancouver. Though her focus is primarily color, she is gradually introducing pattern to her work.*

Two-Layered Scarf

SARAH SAULSON

Finished size: 7½" × 76½" including fringe.

Fabric description: Plain weave, basket weave, and twill.

Warp: Silk, cotton, rayon, and blends (all similar in weight to 10/2 mercerized cotton) painted in gold, turquoise, and magenta.

Weft: 10/2 mercerized cotton in black.

E.P.I.: 22.

Project notes: The two layers of this scarf were woven separately, sewn together, then embellished with handmade tassels. The first layer has a painted warp composed of ten different yarns. Each yarn takes the dye differently, yielding a cloth with rich color variations and depth. The 16-harness threading combines twills, plain weave, and basket weave to create an image of windows. The second layer (not shown) is plain weave. The warp is chenille set at 12 ends per inch and the weft is 10/2 rayon.

Black, White, and Red Scarf

Sarah Saulson

Finished size: 10" × 69" including fringe.

Fabric description: Undulating twill with plain weave.

Warp: Silk, cotton, rayon, and blends (all similar in weight to 10/2 mercerized cotton).

Weft: 2-ply cotton in black.

E.P.I.: 24 for the undulating twill, 20 for the plain weave.

Project notes: This scarf, with its ikat borders, is a direct outgrowth of the influence that ikat from Uzbekistan has had on my designs. I chose an undulating twill because it corresponds so well to the shapes in the ikat design. The scarf's painted warp established a visual dialog with the weave structure, enlarging the scale and repeating the curvilinear form of the twill.

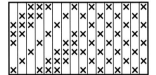

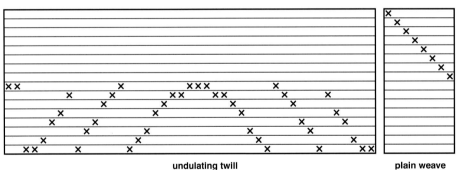

undulating twill   plain weave

Sarah Saulson has been weaving since childhood and established a production weaving studio in the early 1980s. Since 1990, her studio has been the third floor of the old house where she lives in Syracuse, New York. Through her weaving and dyeing she honors and connects with our feminine ancestors who have practiced the fiber arts for eons.

Silk Scarf

Jean Scorgie

Finished size: 7" × 51" including fringe.

Fabric description: Point twill.

Warp and weft: 30/2 silk.

Project notes: Living within driving distance of the Pacific Ocean for many years has given me a fascination for the shells that wash up onto the beaches. These shells, woven in silk with hand-dyed weft and dip-dyed warp on a 16-shaft point twill, are subtly different but equally lovely on each face of the fabric.

Former editor of Handwoven *magazine,* **Jean Scorgie** *enjoys designing fabrics for clothing, especially doubleweaves, with occasional departures into multishaft twills and color-and-weave effects. She lives in Fort Collins, Colorado, with several looms.*

Sunset Blocks

Liz Spear

Finished size: 14" × 97" including fringe.

Fabric description: Block twill.

Warp: 2-ply rayon painted in magenta, lavender, and gold.

Weft: 12/2 cotton in gold.

E.P.I.: 24.

P.P.I.: 20.

Project notes: The warp for this and the following scarf consist of mystery rayon mill ends. I wound each warp in two bundles, A and B, for painting, corresponding to the numbers of ends in the not-quite-random stripes I'd figured for the twill blocks. I love using that structure, in rigidly geometric grids and dot patterns, and these off-balance stripe sequences. I generally use the Fibonacci sequence proportions (1, 2, 3, 5, 8, 13 . . .) with a 4-, 8-, or 12-end block as the base unit. In winding the warp I alternated groups of threads from the A bundle with the B bundle. I wove each scarf with a single weft, shifting from block A to block B and back randomly, paying some attention to the colors coming up in each block and the proportion of the blocks amid the stripes in the warp.

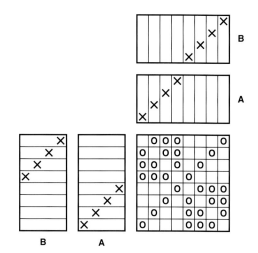

Stripes

LIZ SPEAR

Finished size: 14½" × 103½" including fringe.

Fabric description: Block twill.

Warp: 2-ply rayon painted in magenta, purple, orange, and blue.

Weft: 12/2 cotton in gray-blue.

E.P.I.: 24.

P.P.I.: 20.

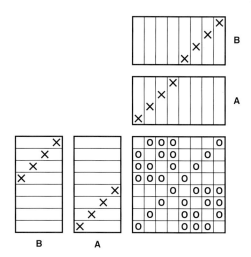

Gray Stripes

LIZ SPEAR

Finished size: 16" × 93" including fringe.

Fabric description: Block twill.

Warp: Selection of yarns in gray, gold, and dip-dyed stripes of sage green, gray, and blue-gray.

E.P.I.: 20.

P.P.I.: 16.

Project notes: This scarf is an overdye color study. I used a block twill threading, with the block changes corresponding to the warp stripes. The dyed warp stripes were wound as a single bundle, using 8 different light blue and light gray yarns in cotton and rayon: 6/2 mercerized, a slub, 8/3, and 16/2. The warp bundle was dip-dyed in a sage green and a grayed turquoise. This particular scarf ended up about half the turquoise color, sliding into the base, and light blue-gray, with a bit of sage at the other end for a border.

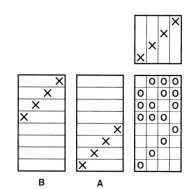

Liz Spear is a full-time craftsperson in western North Carolina, weaving and sewing classic garments for men and women. Her crafts' community includes Penland School and several craft organizations, from which she gains friends, feedback, sales opportunities, and continuing inspiration.

Boulevard Weave Scarf

Yvonne Stahl

Finished size: 7" × 67" including fringe.

Fabric description: Plain weave with supplementary warp.

Warp and weft: 16/2 silk in black (with gold at the selvedges).

Supplementary warp: 16/2 silk in turquoise, lilac, blue, fuchsia, and gold.

E.P.I.: 30.

Project notes: The gold yarn plays a part both in the background, as every second warp end on shaft 2 in the selvedges, and as supplementary warp on shaft 3. The other supplementary warp colors are threaded on shafts 4, 5, and 6.

● = supplementary warp

Pleated Colors

Yvonne Stahl

Finished size: 7" × 78½" including fringe.

Fabric description: Block twill.

Warp: 30/2 silk in white, pink, orange, yellow, dark lavender, dark red, copper, and gray.

Weft: 54/2 high-twist, worsted wool in white.

E.P.I.: 30.

Project notes: The warp is made up of stripes of white silk (block A threading) alternating with colored stripes (block B threading). The scarf begins with short lengths of treadling blocks A and B. I treadled the body of the scarf in block A with short lengths of block B and block A at each end. When I dropped the finished fabric in water and mild detergent for finishing, the pleats formed before my eyes.

Pastel Stripes

YVONNE STAHL

Finished size: 10½" × 85" including fringe.

Fabric description: Crackle weave.

Warp: 30/2 silk in white with random ends of dyed ribbon and dyed yarn.

Tabby Weft: 60/2 silk.

Pattern Weft: 30/2 silk.

Project notes: The crackle blocks are threaded randomly across the warp but always with the incidental between to preserve the twill order. The treadling includes a fine tabby weft throughout. While weaving the scarf, I repeated each treadle of the block sequence a random number of times before moving on to the next treadle of the block.

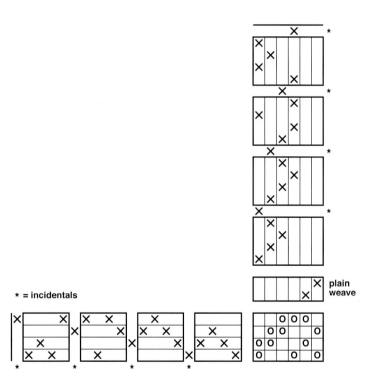

* = incidentals

*Before marriage, **Yvonne Stahl** was a practicing chemical engineer. Because she loves color and design, eighteen years ago, after her children were grown, she took up weaving.*

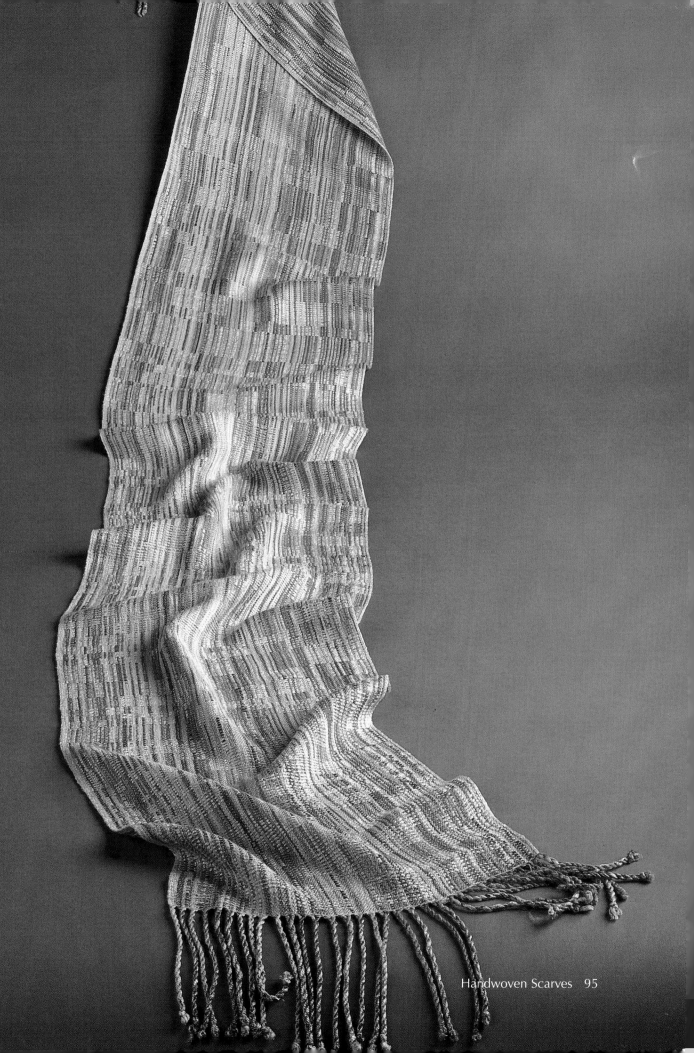

Twill Stars

Vicki Tardy

Finished size: 9" × 70" including fringe.

Fabric description: Twill color-and-weave.

Warp and weft: 2-ply, handspun llama in natural black and red-brown.

E.P.I.: 16.

P.P.I.: 16.

Project notes: This was my first project using handspun llama wool from my own herd, and it proved to be one of the most satisfying projects I have woven in recent years. The natural black and red-brown provide a rich contrast to one another, and the pattern, Twill Stars, immediately came to mind as one that would show these colors to advantage.

X = light
● = dark

Indigo Fancy Point Twill Scarf

VICKI TARDY

Finished size: 9" × 72" including fringe.

Fabric description: Point twill.

Warp: 18/2 wool/silk blend in black.

Weft: 18/2 wool/silk blend in indigo.

E.P.I.: 24.

P.P.I.: 24.

Project notes: I'm always intrigued by the intricacies of fancy twills and by the interaction of colors that are close in value. This scarf satisfied both fascinations and was fun besides.

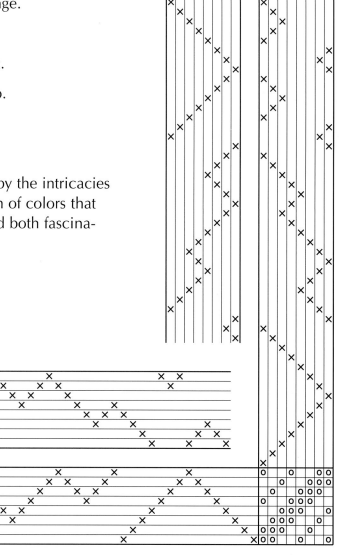

*Teaching weaving has been **Vicki Tardy**'s main focus in recent years. She teaches beginning and intermediate classes, seminars, and workshops in her home studio, at conferences, and for guilds throughout the country. She enjoys exploring various 4- and 8-shaft pattern weaves and adapting them to use in garments and functional household items.*

Angora and Silk Scarf

Pat Wagner Thompson

Finished size: 8½" × 73" including fringe.

Fabric description: Herringbone twill.

Warp and weft: 2-ply handspun silk/angora blend.

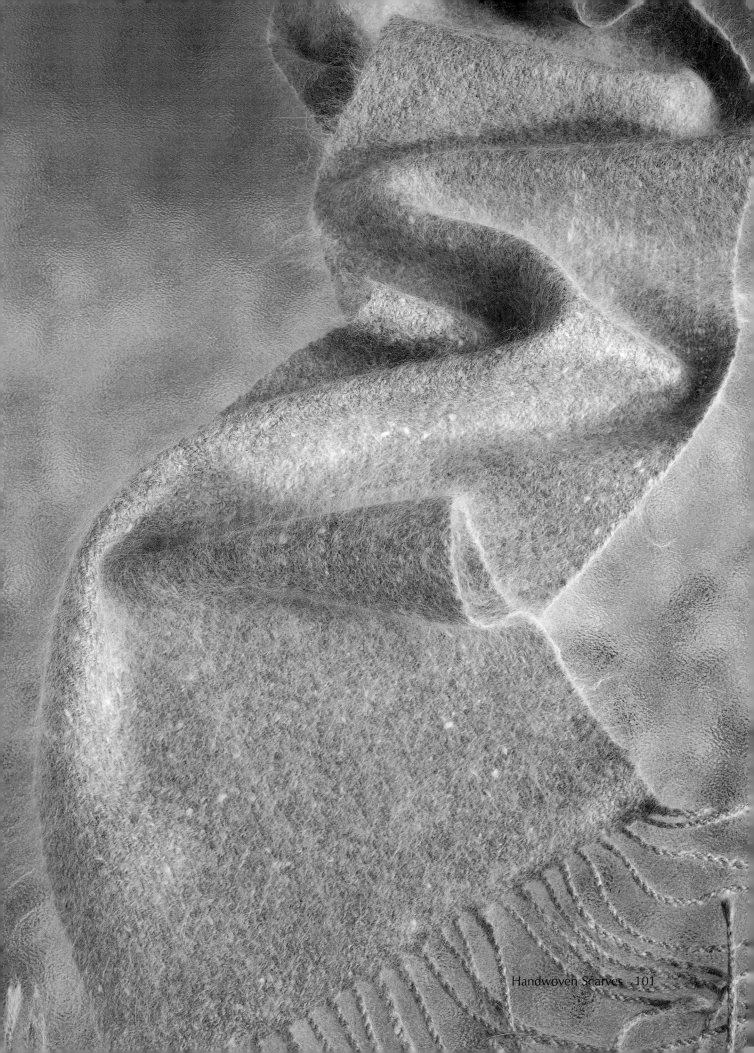

Southern Lights

PAT WAGNER THOMPSON

Finished size: 9" × 70".

Fabric description: Twill.

Warp: 3-ply handspun silk in two weights.

Weft: 3-ply handspun silk.

Project notes: Three different hand-painted silk tops make up the three-ply yarn for this scarf. I spun the warp in two different weights then made stripes of them in the warp.

Pat Wagner Thompson is a real-estate professional, but weaving is her passion. She has been weaving for seventeen years and enjoys weaving one-of-a-kind pieces from her handspun.

Huck Lace Ogee Scarf

LILLIAN WHIPPLE

Finished size: 8" × 72".

Fabric description: Huck lace.

Warp and weft: 220/2 silk in off-white; gold and silver sewing thread.

E.P.I.: 75.

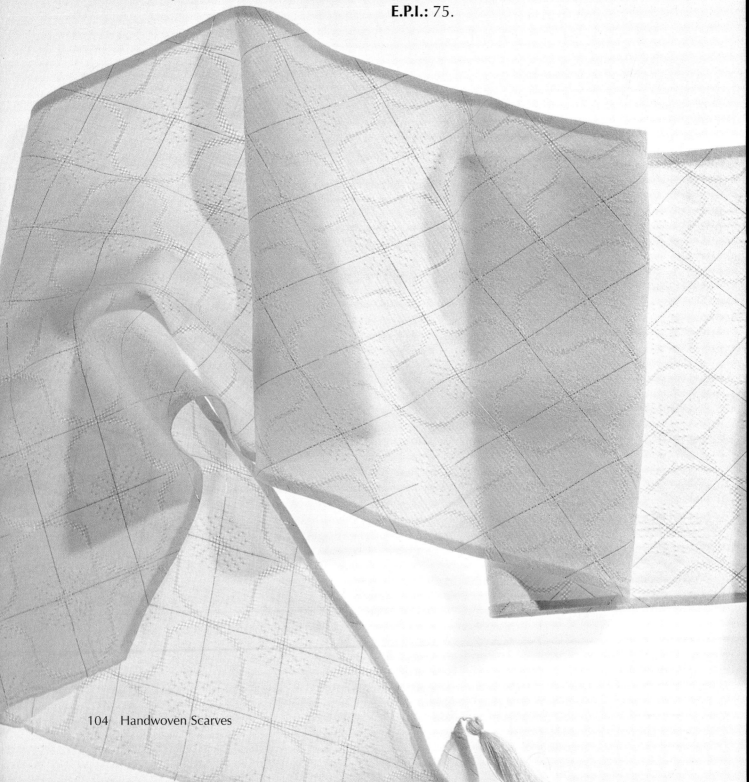

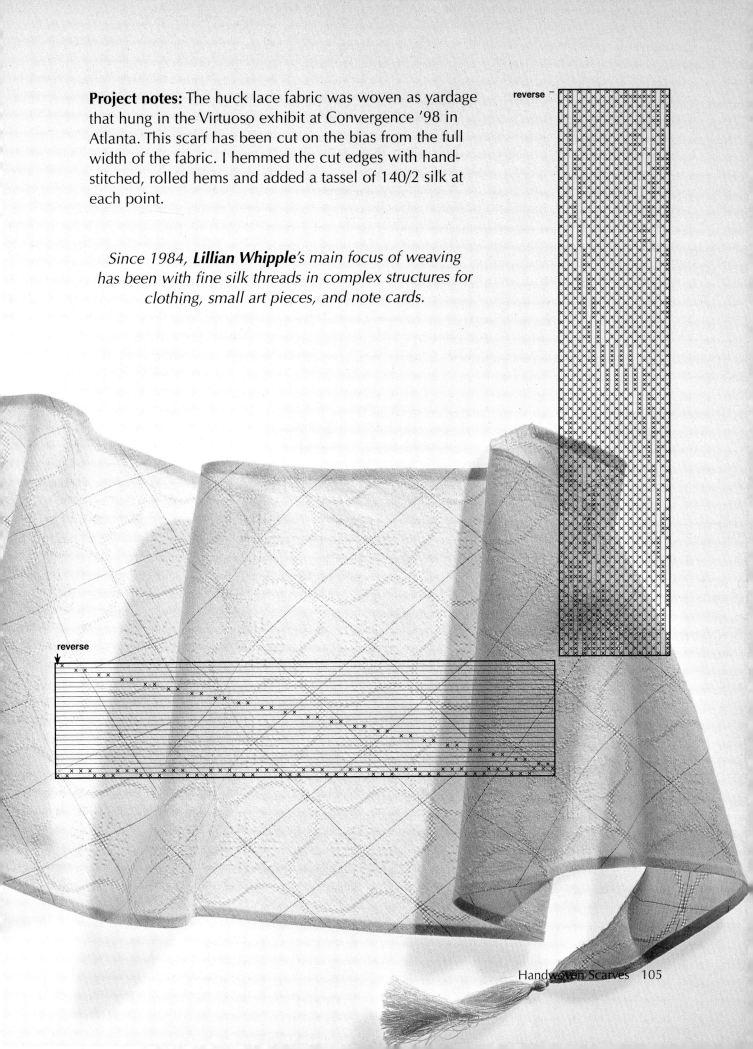

Project notes: The huck lace fabric was woven as yardage that hung in the Virtuoso exhibit at Convergence '98 in Atlanta. This scarf has been cut on the bias from the full width of the fabric. I hemmed the cut edges with hand-stitched, rolled hems and added a tassel of 140/2 silk at each point.

*Since 1984, **Lillian Whipple**'s main focus of weaving has been with fine silk threads in complex structures for clothing, small art pieces, and note cards.*

reverse

reverse

Large Plaid

Michele Wipplinger

Finished size: 22" × 97" including fringe.

Fabric description: Block twill.

Warp and weft: 8/2 silk with occasional silk ribbons
and silk bouclé.

E.P.I.: 24.

Project notes: The warp and weft for the scarf were
hand-painted with natural dyes.

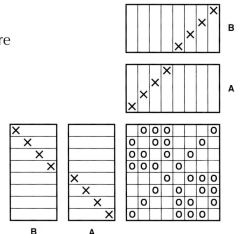

*Michele Wipplinger is president of Color Trends, published author, and leading
colorist, dyer, and textile designer. Through her twenty years of international work,
Michele has compiled a comprehensive body of knowledge on the exquisite
colors of nature and how best to apply them.*

Checkerboard Scarves

Kim Yost Merck

Finished size: *left* 8½" × 79", *right* 9" × 69½".

Fabric description: Block twill.

Warp: 10/2 cotton and 10/2 spun rayon, in white and dip-dyed colors.

Weft: Tussah silk in black.

E.P.I.: 30.

P.P.I.: 32.

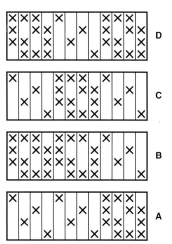

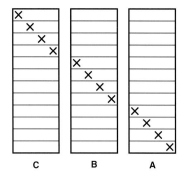

Kim Yost Merck has been a production weaver for the past ten years and has focused on handwoven and dyed scarves exclusively for the last five. She sells her scarves through galleries and selected craft shows including the Smithsonian Craft Show, the Philadelphia Museum of Art Craft Show, and ACC Baltimore. She grew up in a family of artists but made a detour into engineering before discovering weaving.

Wrap Around

NELL ZNAMIEROWSKI

Finished size: 21" × 102".

Fabric description: Plain weave.

Warp and weft: Wool singles in purple, turquoise, magenta, rust, yellow, and dark red.

E.P.I.: 10.

P.P.I.: 9.

Nell Znamierowski is a textile designer and color consultant who recently retired from the Fashion Institute of Technology in New York City where she taught woven design. She has also taught countless workshops in the United States, Canada, Mexico, and Italy. A graduate of the Rhode Island School of Design, she also studied in Finland on a Fulbright Fellowship. She is the author of Step-By-Step Weaving *and has contributed articles to* Handwoven, American Craft, *and* Piecework. *Her fiber art is in the collections of the Renwick and The Art Institute of Chicago.*

Index

This index consists of weavings by name in italics, and page containing each weaver's biography.